Teachers

Jokes, Quotes, and Anecdotes

Teachers

Jokes, Quotes, and Anecdotes

Edited by Patrick Regan

STARK BOOKS

Andrews McMeel Publishing

Kansas City

ISBN: 0-7407-1403-1

Library of Congress Catalog Card Number: 00-108469

Book design by Holly Camerlinck
Illustrations by Deborah Zemke

A teacher affects eternity; he can never tell where his influence stops.

—Henry Brooks Adams

How many of us can say our work positively affects the lives of hundreds or even thousands of others? For teachers, their work, their careers, most certainly do. The gravity of this is the source of pressure teachers feel every day, yet it is also their greatest pride and motivation.

Why teach? The stresses are legion, the salaries notoriously low, and, as any teacher weary from a late night of grading tests and preparing lesson plans will tell you, the workday stretches far beyond the ringing of the three o'clock bell. So, why teach? An old educator's joke says there are only three good reasons: June, July, and August. But the real reason is probably because there are those who simply have to teach. Teaching is not a job. It is a calling.

Those called to teach know their success doesn't rest on pushing their charges through lesson after lesson, year after year, but rather on instilling in their students a hunger to learn. Teachers have students for only a short time. They must inspire them in ways that go far beyond the successful navigation of the math equation on the blackboard—in ways that students themselves likely won't realize until their school days are a memory.

Just as good teachers inspire students, this noble and sometimes nutty profession itself inspires insightful, witty, and wry comments from writers, statesmen, celebrities, humorists—and, of course, teachers. This entertaining little

book includes hundreds of clever jokes, quotes, and anec-
dotes about teachers, students, schools, and teaching. Pay
close attention . . . you just might learn something.

—Patrick Regan

A teacher's day is one-half bureaucracy, one-half crisis, one-half monotony, and one-eightieth epiphany. Never mind the arithmetic.

—*Susan Ohanian*

When a teacher calls a boy by his entire name it means trouble.

—*Mark Twain*

Nothing grieves a child more than
to study the wrong lesson and learn something
he wasn't supposed to.

— *E. C. McKenzie*

Some kids want to know why the
teachers get paid when it's the kids
who have to do all the work!

— *Milton Berle*

A little boy worrying through his very first day at school raised his hand for permission to go to the washroom, then returned to the class a few moments later to report that he couldn't find it. Dispatched a second time with explicit directions, he still couldn't find it. So this time the teacher asked a slightly older boy to act as guide. Success crowned his efforts. "We finally found it," the older boy told the teacher. "He had his pants on backward."

—*Bennett Cerf*

CRAZY THINGS KIDS WRITE ON TESTS:

A virgin forest is a bunch of trees where the hand of man hasn't set foot.

The spinal column is a long bunch of bones. The head sits on the top and you sit on the bottom.

The difference between a king
and a president is that a king is the son
of his father, but a president isn't.

In spring, the salmon swim upstream
to spoon.

TEACHER: "Please write a story in the first
person."
STUDENT: "Does that mean to write it just like
Adam woulda done?"

—*James E. Myers*

Smartness runs in my family.
When I went to school I was so smart
my teacher was in my class for five years.

—*Gracie Allen*

Everywhere I go I'm asked if I think the university stifles writers. My opinion is that they don't stifle enough of them. There's many a bestseller that could have been prevented by a good teacher.

—Flannery O'Connor

The real menace in dealing with a five-year-old is that in no time at all you begin to sound like a five-year-old.

—Jean Kerr

I have three kids in school . . . and they were all talking about how they had studied Martin Luther King. The kindergartner was telling me that black people had to sit in the back of the bus, way back when. I asked my first-grader, "Why do you think black people had to sit in the back of the bus?" She had no idea . . . so I asked my third-grader. . . . He said, "Well, I think back then, some white people were really buttheads." Out of the mouths of babes, huh?

—*Daniel Kelly*, Warning! Cute Kid Stories Ahead!

"That's the reason they're called lessons,"
the Gryphon remarked, "because they
lesson from day to day."

—*Lewis Carroll*, Alice in Wonderland

Education is wonderful—it helps you worry
about things all over the world.

—*Joey Adams*

While teaching at the preschool level, I was cleaning out shelves one day. I held up some 45-rpm records that I found. One of the boys quickly announced that he also had some CD-ROMS at home! A sign of the times!

—*Carol Fox*

In elementary school, many a true word is spoken in guess.

—*Henny Youngman*

A certain young man came home with a grievously unsatisfactory report card in January. "Oh, dear," said his mother, "what is the trouble?"

"There isn't any trouble," said the youngster. "You know how it is yourself; things are always marked down after the holidays."

—*Edmund Fuller*

A good education is the next best thing
to a pushy mother.

—Charles Schulz, Peanuts

It is hard to convince a high school student
that he will encounter a lot of problems more
difficult than those of algebra and geometry.

—Edgar W. Howe

A young boy ran up to his teacher with tears in his eyes. The teacher asked, "What's wrong, dear?" The boy said, "I just found out I'll be in school until I'm eighteen." The teacher said, "That's not a problem. I have to stay here until I'm sixty-five!"

—*Milton Berle*

Students at a Chicago grade school christened their drinking fountain "Old Faceful."

—*James E. Myers*

A new teacher, trying to make use of her psychology courses, started her class by saying, "Everyone who thinks you're stupid, stand up."

After a few seconds, little Johnny stood up. The teacher said, "Do you think you're stupid, Johnny?"

"No Ma'am," he said, "but I hate to see you standing up there all by yourself."

—*Loyal Jones*

I was raised in a small town called Critz
[Virginia]. It was so small that our school
taught driver's education and sex education
in the same car.

—*Mary Sue Terry*

Good teaching is one-fourth preparation
and three-fourths theater.

—*Gail Godwin*

Learning, *n.* The kind of ignorance affected by (and affecting) civilized races, as distinguished from ignorance, the sort of learning incurred by savages. See **nonsense.**

—*Ambrose Bierce*

The true teacher defends his pupils against his own personal influence.

—*A. B. Alcott*

My teacher has a reading problem.
He can't read my writing.

—Leopold Fechtner

Education is simply the soul of a society as it
passes from one generation to another.

—G. K. Chesterton

A school kid asks his teacher, "Is it true that
the law of gravity keeps us on Earth?"
The teacher says, "Yes."
The kid asks, "What kept us before
the law was passed?"

—*Milton Berle*

The schools ain't what they used to be
and never was.

—*Will Rogers*

Some students drink at the fountain
of knowledge. Others just gargle.

—*E. C. McKenzie*

I'm not rushing into being in love.
I'm finding fourth grade hard enough.

—*Regina, age ten*

—Bart Simpson

Charming women can true converts make,
We love the precepts for the teacher's sake.

—George Farquhar

She was only a schoolteacher's daughter—but
she certainly taught me a lesson.

—*Joey Adams*

The decent docent doesn't doze;
He teaches standing on his toes.
His student dassn't doze and does,
And that's what teaching is and was.

—*David McCord, "What Cheer"*

Teacher's True Story

I was teaching four little kids how to play Go Fish, and the luck of the draw just wasn't with little Jimmy. After losing the third game in a row the red-faced boy protested, "I don't like this game—it's not fair!" I tried to explain that he should learn how to be a good loser. He retorted, "You're the teacher—when are you going to teach me to *win!*"

—*Jim Stringer*

When I was in school, one of my teachers was crazy about me. I once heard her tell another teacher, "I wish he was my kid for one day!"

—*Milton Berle*

Education is not filling a pail but the lighting of a fire.

—*William Butler Yeats*

TEACHER: "Emil, give me the formula for water,
plain water."

EMIL: "I, J, K, L, M, N, O."

TEACHER: "Emil! You know that's not right!"

EMIL: "I was certain that it was. Didn't you
say the formula was H to O?"

—James E. Myers

In the sixth grade they wanted me to count up
to ten—from memory.

—Henny Youngman

Grammar school never taught me anything
about grammar.

—*Isaac Goldberg*

TEACHER: (answering the telephone) "You
say Billy Smith has a bad cold
and can't come to school? Who is
this speaking?"
VOICE: (with assumed hoarseness) "This is
my father."

—*Lewis and Faye Copeland*

I wonder whether if I had had an education
I should have been more or less a fool
than I am.

—*Alice James,* The Diary of Alice James

"Son, I'm worried about your being
at the bottom of the class."
"Pop, they teach the same stuff at both ends!"

—*Milton Berle*

Small children start to school these days with
a big advantage. They already know
two letters of the alphabet—TV.

—*E. C. McKenzie*

Children of Distinction: The promising seven-
year-old was given the difficult assignment in
class of describing the taste of chocolate ice
cream in a single sentence. "Chocolate," she
explained, "tastes the opposite of vanilla."

—*Bennett Cerf*

Little Tommy was in the first grade. One day, he came home and his mother asked: "Well, Tommy, what did you learn in school today?"

"In arithmetic, I learned that three and three make seven."

"But that's not correct," his mother said.

"Well, then, I guess I didn't learn anything."

—*James E. Myers*

Education is what survives when what has
been learned has been forgotten.

—*B. F. Skinner*

PROFESSOR: "This essay on your dog is, word for
word, the same as your brother's."
STUDENT: "Yes, sir, it's the same dog."

—*Mildred Meiers and Jack Knapp*

Schoolmasters and parents exist to be
grown out of.

—*John Wolfenden*

I had to go to school to see my kid's guidance
counselor. They told me my kid was out; he'd
be back in one to three years.

—*Rodney Dangerfield*

Mr. Clemenceau posted a sign in the classroom stating, "Because of a conference, Mr. Clemenceau will not teach his classes tomorrow."

One of his smart-alecky pupils erased the "c" in classes.

Up to such student shenanigans, Mr. Clemenceau erased the "l."

—*James E. Myers*

I will not call my teacher "Hot Cakes."
I will not call my teacher "Hot Cakes."
I will not call my teacher "Hot . . .

—*Bart Simpson*

Once I'm done with kindergarten,
I'm going to find me a wife.

—*Tommy, age five*

Education will broaden a narrow mind, but
there is no known cure for a big head.

—*J. Graham*

Let schoolmasters puzzle the brain,
With grammar, and nonsense, and learning,
Good liquor, I stoutly maintain,
Gives genius a better discerning.

—*Oliver Goldsmith, "She Stoops to Conquer"*

[The shortage of student loans] may require . . . divestiture of certain sorts—stereo divestiture, automobile divestiture, three-weeks-at-the-beach divestiture.

—*William J. Bennett*

The perfect method of learning is analogous to infection. It enters and spreads.

—*Leo Stein*

One week I had four high school students mistakenly call me "Mom." Sometimes when they need help on a project, they call out "Mom" instead of "Miss." They are mortified when they call me Mom—everyone laughs, they get embarrassed, and I give them extra credit!

—*Cindy Maguire*

I just read about a schoolteacher
who got hurt. She was grading papers
on a curve!

—*Milton Berle*

Those that do teach young babes
Do it with gentle means and easy tasks.

—*William Shakespeare*, Othello

I'm a retired schoolteacher. . . . My favorite classroom story concerns a young third-grade girl who came to school one morning all excited. She explained that things were really different at their house now because her grandfather had come to live with them. Then, she said, "And he's sterile, you know!" The teacher thought for a moment and then replied, "You mean senile, don't you?" The child replied, "That too."

—*Daniel Kelly,* Warning! Cute Kid Stories Ahead!

I am teaching . . . It's kind of like having a love affair with a rhinoceros.

—*Anne Sexton*

At a conference on education, a vote-conscious state senator boomed from the speaker's platform, "Long live our teachers!" From the back of the hall came the query, "On what?"

—*Bennett Cerf*

Quite frankly, teachers are the only profession
that teach our children.

—*Dan Quayle*

It is noble to teach oneself, but still nobler to
teach others—and less trouble.

—*Mark Twain*

When asked for her occupation, a woman charged with a traffic violation said she was a schoolteacher. The judge rose from the bench. "Madam, I have waited years for a schoolteacher to appear before this court," he smiled with delight. "Now sit down at that table and write 'I will not pass through a red light' five hundred times."

I didn't really dislike school. It was the principal of the thing.

—*Henny Youngman*

I am always ready to learn although I do not always like being taught.

—*Winston Churchill*

Excuses at School

Please permit our son, Tom, to miss
school today. He's got diarrhea
and what's more, his boots leak.

—*James E. Myers*

Education helps you earn more.
But not many schoolteachers can prove it.

—E. C. McKenzie

I will not conduct my own fire drills.
I will not conduct my own fire drills.
I will not conduct . . .

—Bart Simpson

I am putting old heads on your young shoulders. All my pupils are the crème de la crème. Give me a girl of an impressionable age, and she is mine for life.

—*Muriel Spark,* The Prime of Miss Jean Brodie

There is no crisis to which academics will not respond with a seminar.

—*Old saying*

It would be a great advantage to some
schoolmasters if they would steal two hours
a day from their pupils, and give their own
minds the benefit of the robbery.

—*J. F. Boyse*

A professor is one who talks
in someone else's sleep.

—*W. H. Auden*

Public schools: A place of detention for
children placed in the care of teachers who
are afraid of the principal, principals who are
afraid of the school board, school boards
who are afraid of the parents, parents who are
afraid of the children, and children who
are afraid of nobody.

—*Anonymous*

The eggs do not teach the hen.

—*Russian proverb*

One thing stopped me from going to college:
high school.

—Henny Youngman

"What is the plural of man, Willie?" asked
the teacher.

"Men," answered Willie.

"And, the plural of child?"

"Twins," was the unexpected reply.

—Lewis and Faye Copeland

I never did very well in math—I could never seem to persuade the teacher that I hadn't meant my answers literally.

—*Calvin Trillin*

Schoolteachers are not fully appreciated by parents until it rains all day Saturday.

—*E. C. McKenzie*

Teaching consists of equal parts perspiration, inspiration, and resignation.

—*Susan Ohanian*

I went to school with a kid who was so smart, the only time he got an answer wrong, they had to go back and change the question.

—*Gene Perret*

ACTUAL WRITTEN EXCUSES
GIVEN TO TEACHERS

"Please excuse Dianne from being absent yesterday. She was in bed with gramps."

"Please excuse Johnnie for being. It was his father's fault."

"Please excuse Ray Friday from school. He has very loose vowels."

Everyone is wise, until he speaks.

—*Irish proverb*

I took a little English, a little math, some science, some hubcaps, and some wheelcovers.

—*Gates Brown*

I once asked a fifth-grader, "Why did you hit Gregory?" The kid answered, "Because he hit me back first."

— *Sam Levenson*

TEACHER: "This is the fourth time you've been so bad that I've had to punish you this week. What do you care to say about your actions?"
STUDENT: "Thank God it's Friday!"

— *James E. Myers*

She used to be a teacher but she has
no class now.

—*Fred Allen*

If you think education is expensive—
try ignorance.

—*Derek Bok*

When I was a kid I never went to school—
I said I was sick—but I always managed to
get better by 3:30—I'd run into the kitchen—
"Look, Ma—a miracle happened! I'm well!
A little angel came and sat on my bed—
she touched me with a wand and said,
'Go out and play.'"

—*Bill Cosby*

I once played hooky from school.
My teacher sent a thank-you note!

—*Milton Berle*

I will not expose the ignorance of the faculty.
I will not expose the ignorance of the faculty.
I will not expose . . .

—*Bart Simpson*

From the examination paper of a nine-year-old
Chicago hopeful named Larry Wolters:
"Nathan Haley said, 'I only regret that I have
but one life to give for my country.' This has
come to be know as Haley's comment."

—Bennett Cerf

My history teacher was so old,
he taught from memory.

—Henny Youngman

Don't despair of a student if he has
one clear idea.

—*Nathanial Emmons*

TEACHER: "Bobby, and how do you like school?"
BOBBY: "When it's closed."

Mothers are great. When I was teaching,
a mother once wrote me a note about
her son. It said, "If Gregory is a bad boy,
don't slap him, slap the boy next to him.
Gregory will get the idea."

—*Sam Levenson*

You have become silly from teaching children!
You have given them what little sense you
have, and they gave you all their stupidity.

—*Joseph Roth*

I work at a day-care center. We were sittin' around yesterday, and a little girl said to me: "My mom told me that she wears my dad's pants in this family."

—*Daniel Kelly,* Warning! Cute Kid Stories Ahead!

In the first place God made idiots. This was for practice. Then he made school boards.

—*Mark Twain*

It was a tough school. The kids on the debating team took steroids!

—*Milton Berle*

It is important that students bring a certain ragamuffin, barefoot irreverence to their studies; they are not here to worship what is known, but to question it.

—*Jacob Bronowski*

TEACHER: "If you subtract fourteen from a hundred sixteen, what's the difference?"

TOMMY: "Yeah, I think it's a lot of foolishness, too."

—Lewis and Faye Copeland

Too often we give children answers to remember rather than problems to solve.

—Roger Lewin

There once was a student named Bessor
Whose knowledge grew lessor and lessor.
It at last grew so small
He knew nothing at all,
And today he's a college professor!

—*Bennett Cerf*

In examinations those who do not wish to
know ask questions of those who cannot tell.

—*Sir Walter Raleigh*

America's future walks through the doors
of our schools each day.

—*Mary Jean Le Tendre*

A student is reprimanded for not having
written a book report on a Dickens novel.
The student says, "I couldn't help it.
We couldn't get the video."

—*Milton Berle*

The teacher asked: "What was the name of the person in Greek mythology who was half man and half animal?" Paul raised his hand. "Yes?" the teacher nodded. "Buffalo Bill!"

—*James E. Myers*

I quit school in the fifth grade because of pneumonia. Not because I had it but because I couldn't spell it.

—*Rocky Graziano*

A young grade school teacher had just handed out report cards and awards to a class of obstreperous brats, and sent them off to their summer vacations. Now she leaned back in her chair and sighed, "I guess teaching school is pretty much like having a baby. Each takes nine months, and the last week is the worst!"

—*Bennett Cerf*

A good education should leave
much to be desired.

— Alan Gregg

Goodbye tension, hello pension!

—Fay Michaud, retiring teacher

The vanity of teaching doth oft tempt
a man to forget that he is a blockhead.

—*George Savile, Marquis of Halifax*

Indeed, one of the ultimate advantages of
education is simply coming to an end of it.

—*B. F. Skinner*

My homework was not stolen by a one-armed man.
My homework was not stolen by a one-armed man.
My homework . . .

—*Bart Simpson*

The object of teaching a child is
to enable him to get along without his teacher.

—*Elbert Hubbard*

Letter Received by an Elementary School Teacher in the Bronx

"Please never hit our Sylvester again. He's a delicate, sensitive boy and is not used to corporal punishment. We never hit him at home except in self-defense."

—*Bennett Cerf*

The pupil was asked to paraphrase the sentence, "He was bent on seeing her." He wrote, "The sight of her doubled him up."

—Lewis and Faye Copeland

Some professors feel the reason the modern student doesn't burn the midnight oil as he used to is that he doesn't get in soon enough.

—Mildred Meiers and Jack Knapp

A kindergarten teacher has to know how to
make the little things count.

—*Henny Youngman*

A toast to the Graduate—in a class by himself.

—*Paul Dickson*

A North Carolina school committeeman informed his neighbor that the school board had decided not to renew the contract of the man who taught science at the high school. The neighbor expressed his surprise, saying he understood that this particular teacher had attended many colleges and earned many degrees. The school committeeman replied, "That's the trouble with him. He has been educated way past his intelligence."

—Senator Sam J. Ervin Jr.

"The teacher said I must learn to write more legibly," the kid told his mother, "but if I do, she'll find out I can't spell."

—*Joey Adams*

The first-grader was talking about the recent fire in his school. "I knew it was going to happen," he said. "We had been practicing for it all year."

—*Harry B. Otis*

I forget what I was taught.
I only remember what I have learned.

—*Patrick White*

If you can't do, teach. If you can't teach,
teach phys. ed.

—*Anonymous*

The ten-year-old son of the richest, most humorless codger in town was a first-rate, four-star, all-American cheat, but the teacher hesitated to snitch on him to the old man. Finally, she compromised on this note: "Judging by his recent written exams, your son is forging his way continuously ahead."

—*Bennett Cerf*

The college graduate is presented with a
sheepskin to cover his intellectual nakedness.

—*Robert M. Hutchins*

Treat a man as he is and he will remain as he
is. Treat a man as he can and should be and he
will become as he can and should be.

—*Johann Wolfgang von Goethe*

My four-year-old asked if his best friend, a five-year-old girl, could spend the night. I said she could. Shortly after she arrived they began to fight, so I stepped in and insisted they apologize and make up. When my son refused, his friend said, "Well, I guess this means I have to sleep on the couch!"

—www.becquet.com

A great teacher never strives to explain his vision. He simply invites you to stand beside him and see for yourself.

—*R. Inman*

We judge ourselves by what we feel capable of doing, while others judge us by what we have done.

—*Henry Wadsworth Longfellow*

Life is what happens while you are
making other plans.

—*John Lennon*

PERRY: "Summer vacation. Wow! I plan to
do nothing for the next three
months."

TEACHER: "That should be easy, Perry. You've
been practicing for nine months!"

—*James E. Myers*

If, in instructing a child, you are vexed
with it for want of adroitness, try, if you have
never tried before, to write with your left
hand, and then remember that a child is
all left hand.

—*J. F. Boyse*

Old teachers never die, they just grade away.

—*Henny Youngman*

God forgive me for having thought it possible
that a schoolmaster could be out and out a
rational being.

—*Sir Walter Scott*

Teachers at all levels encourage the idea that
you have to talk about things in order to
understand them, because they wouldn't have
jobs, otherwise. But it's phony, you know.

—*Denise Levertov,* The Craft of Poetry

I never graduated from Iowa. I was only there for two terms—Truman's and Eisenhower's.

— Alex Karras

TEACHER: "Is it correct to say, 'You have et'?"

JOHNNY: "No, it's wrong."

TEACHER: "Why is it wrong to say, 'You have et'?"

JOHNNY: "Because I ain't et yet."

All a youngster wants out of school is himself.

—*E. C. Mckenzie*

The human brain is special. It starts working
as soon as you get up, and it doesn't stop
until you get to school.

—*Milton Berle*

I once wrote an essay in college, and it read: "The woman fell and lay prostitute on the ground."

The professor's note of correction read: "The word you want is 'prostrate.' There is a difference between a fallen woman and one who has temporarily slipped."

—Susan of Bayfield, Wisconsin (Daniel Kelly,
The Best of Bulletin Board*)*

The teacher should never lose his temper in the presence of the class. If a man, he may take refuge in profane soliloquies; if a woman, she may follow the example of one sweet-faced and apparently tranquil girl—go out in the yard and gnaw a post.

—*William Lyon Phelps,* Teaching in School and College

Let such teach others who themselves excel, And censure freely who have written well.

—*Alexander Pope*

Education can get you the only thing
that really matters in today's world—
an assigned parking space.

—Gene Perret

TEACHER: "Tommy, where was the Declaration
of Independence signed?"
TOMMY: "At the bottom, I guess."

Teacher's True Story

When trying unsuccessfully to put on
his tennis shoes, one of my boys said,
"My elbows are too big for these shoes!"
Of course, he meant his heels!

—*Donna O'Briant*

I went pretty far as far as school goes—
four blocks.

—*Henny Youngman*

Common to all staff was a conviction that they
could have done better outside education.
The teachers believed in a mysterious world
outside the school called "business"
where money was handed out freely.

—*Michael Green*, The Boy Who Shot Down an Airship

Education: A succession of eye-openers each involving the repudiation of some previously held belief.

—*George Bernard Shaw*

My education was dismal. I went to a series of schools for mentally disturbed teachers.

—*Woody Allen*

The schoolkids in some towns are getting so
tough that teachers are playing hooky.

—*E. C. McKenzie*

I will not go near the kindergarten turtle.
I will not go near the kindergarten turtle.
I will not go near the kinder . . .

—*Bart Simpson*

I am inclined to think that one's education has been in vain if one fails to learn that most schoolmasters are idiots.

— *Hesketh Pearson*

There is now less flogging in our great schools than formerly, but then less is learned there; so that what the boys get at one end they lose at the other.

— *Samuel Johnson*

TEACHER: "Stanley, every day since school began you have been late. Why?"

STANLEY: "It's not my fault! There's a sign at almost every crossing that says, 'go slow'!"

—*James E. Myers*

It is better to perish than to continue schoolmastering.

—*Thomas Caryle*

TEACHER: "What do you call the last teeth we
get?"
PUPIL: "False teeth."

—Lewis and Faye Copeland

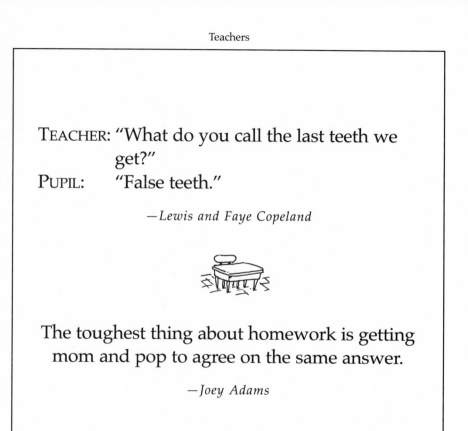

The toughest thing about homework is getting
mom and pop to agree on the same answer.

—Joey Adams

A teacher was asked to fill out a special questionnaire for the state. One question said, "Give two reasons for entering the teaching profession." The teacher wrote, "July and August."

—*Milton Berle*

A teacher should be sparing of his smile.

—*William Cowper*

[My son] was at preschool screening and
the instructor held up a colored card and
asked him, "What color is this?" And he said,
"Why? Don't you know?"

—*Daniel Kelly,* Warning! Cute Kid Stories Ahead!

No wonder the teacher knows so much;
she has the book.

—*Edgar Watson Howe*

To me education is a leading out of what is already there in the pupil's soul. To Miss Mackay it is a putting in of something that is not there, and that is not what I call education, I call it intrusion.

—*Muriel Spark,* The Prime of Miss Jean Brodie

If falling in love is anything like learning to spell, I don't want to do it. It takes too long to learn.

—*Leo, age seven*

I'd like to say a few words about one of the most popular concepts in modern education— show and tell. Show and tell is a device created by grammar schools to communicate family secrets to thirty-two other families before 9:15 in the morning!

—*Robert Orben*

From facing down rattlesnakes in broom
closets with the spring thaw to fending off
ranchhand bullies (or lovelorn cowboys),
teachers had to be wise in the ways
of the world.

—*Jim Bencivenga, "On Country Schools"*

MOTHER: "What did you learn in school
today, Clarence?"
CLARENCE: "How to whisper without moving
my lips."

—*Mildred Meiers and Jack Knapp*

When I was teaching school in Brooklyn, one of my assignments was Hall Patrol. During one of my routine checks of the staircases, I found this big fifteen-year-old fondly squeezing the life out of an attractive young lady. I pulled him away angrily. "What on earth do you think you're doing?" Without even so much as a blush he came back with, "It's okay, Mr. Levenson, she lives on my block."

—Sam Levenson

I have never let my schooling interfere
with my education.

— Mark Twain

You can get help from teachers, but you are
going to have to learn a lot by yourself,
sitting alone in a room.

— Theodore Geisel (Dr. Seuss)

True terror is to wake up one morning
and discover that your high school class
is running the country.

—*Kurt Vonnegut*

A Minneapolis, Minnesota, high school
teacher hung this sign under the clock in
her classroom: "Time will pass . . . will you?"

—*James E. Myers*

It's Charlotte Bradford's notion that schoolteachers petition for higher salaries at the
wrong time of the year. "If they'd wait till
the beginning of August—just past halfway
in the kids' summer vacations—to make their
plea, parents would give them anything
they asked on the first ballot!"

— *Bennett Cerf*

No one can look back on his schooldays
and say with truth that they were
altogether unhappy.

—*George Orwell*

The teacher's life is painfull and therefore
would be pityed: it wrastles with
unthankfulnesse above all measure . . .
Our calling creepes low and hath pain
for companion.

—*Richard Mulcaster*

The chief wonder of education is that it does not ruin everybody concerned in it, teachers and taught.

—*Henry Adams*

A country school board had a teacher prospect in to size him up. One member asked him whether the earth was round or flat. He didn't bat an eye. "I don't know how you people feel about it, but I can teach it either way."

—*Dr. Eslie Asbury*

Teacher's True Story

Two girls and a boy were having a pretend wedding. One girl was the preacher, the other wore a bride doll's wedding dress on her head, and the boy carried a play wallet. After hearing the preacher say, "I now pronounce you man and wife," I expected to hear "You may now kiss the bride." Imagine my surprise when I heard, "The groom may now put his wallet in the bride's purse."

—*Martha Gillham*

Education is the period during which you
are being instructed by somebody you do
not know, about something you do not
want to know.

—*G. K. Chesterton*

I was—but am no more, thank God—
a schoolteacher. I dreamed last night I was
teaching again—that's the only bad dream
that ever afflicts my sturdy conscience.

—*D. H. Lawrence*

A grade school teacher was instructing her youngsters on the value of coins. She took a half-dollar and laid it on her desk. "Can any of you tell me what it is?" she asked.

From the rear of the room came the shrill voice of a small boy, "Tails!"

—*Harry B. Otis*

A schoolmaster should have an atmosphere of awe, and walk wonderingly, as if he was amazed at being himself.

—*Walter Bagehot*

The kids in my old neighborhood never drop out of school. There'd be nobody to drive the teachers crazy.

—*Milton Berle*

TEACHER: "Which is farther away, England or the Moon?"

JOHNNY: "England."

TEACHER: "England? What makes you think that?"

JOHNNY: "'Cause we can see the Moon and we can't see England."

—*Lewis and Faye Copeland*

I would rather fail in a cause that someday
will triumph, than to win in a cause
that I know will someday fail.

—*Woodrow Wilson*

You got to be careful if you don't
know where you're going, because you
might not get there.

—*Yogi Berra*

Junior was being chided for his low grades. Little Robert, who lived a few doors away, was held up as an example.

"Robert doesn't get C's and D's does he?" asked his father.

"No," Junior admitted, "but he's different. He has very bright parents."

—*Jacob M. Braude*

One morning as I was teaching a Grade 2 class, Andy arrived at school in an excited mood. His family had just acquired a new dog, and he was bubbling over in his description of their new pet. "What color is your dog?" I asked. Without hesitation he answered, "Pitch white!"

—www.becquet.com

I've always tried to be aware of what I say
in my films, because all of us who make
motion pictures are teachers—teachers
with very loud voices.

—*George Lucas*

A teacher is a person who used to think
he liked children.

—*Joey Adams*

A man should keep his little brain attic
stocked with all the furniture that he is likely
to use, and the rest he can put away in
the lumber room of his library, where
he can get it if he wants it.

—*Arthur Conan Doyle*

A good teacher feels his way,
looking for response.

—*Paul Goodman*, Growing Up Absurd

Training is everything. The peach was once
a bitter almond; cauliflower is nothing but
cabbage with a college education.

—*Mark Twain*

Teachers can change lives with just the
right mix of chalk and challenges.

—*Joyce A Myers*

[A kindergarten teacher] was helping one of her students choose the child's best schoolwork for a portfolio to give to the first-grade teacher. After the kindergarten teacher encouraged the child to "put her best foot forward," the little girl asked, "What should I do with my other foot?"

—*Daniel Kelly*, Warning! Cute Kid Stories Ahead!

The principal's toupee is not a Frisbee.
The principal's toupee is not a Frisbee.
The principal's toupee is not . . .

—Bart Simpson

TEACHER: "Tommy, what is a synonym?"
TOMMY: "A synonym is a word you use
             when you can't spell the other one."

—Mildred Meiers and Jack Knapp

No other job in the world could possibly
dispossess one so completely as this job of
teaching. You could stand all day in a laundry,
for instance, still in possession of your mind.
But this teaching utterly obliterates you.
It cuts right into your being: essentially, it
takes over your spirit. It drags it out
from where it would hide.

—*Sylvia Ashton-Warner*

Teacher's True Story

One night at the dinner table, my four-year-old son asked me if "ridiculous" was a bad word. I said, "No," but he explained how he got in trouble for using it at day care: "Today Travis pushed me, and I didn't like it, so I pushed him back. The teacher came over and asked who pushed first. Travis said I did, but that's not the truth, so I said 'He's, he's . . . he's diclous!'"

—*Dave Thompson*

A substitute teacher in a downtown public school surveyed her class the first morning she was assigned a job and sent a hurry call for the principal. "Help!" she demanded. "They're all here!"

—*Bennett Cerf*

I started in school in the first grade. Years passed, but I didn't.

—*Henny Youngman*

Muffy of Stillwater is still reminiscing about her daughter's second day of kindergarten. She looked up at me and said, "Why are you crying, Mom?"

I said, "Oh, I'm just kinda sad, 'cause my baby's going to school."

And she said, "Don't be sad. This is a whole new life for me."

—*Daniel Kelly,* The Best of Bulletin Board

A little fellow in the second grade remarked, "I ain't got no pencil, teacher."

The teacher groaned and said to him, "It's 'I don't have a pencil'—you don't have a pencil—we don't have any pencils—they don't have any pencils. Now, do you understand that?"

"Not really," the kid replied. "Tell me . . . what happened to all them pencils?"

—*James E. Myers*

When I came home and showed my mother
my report card with a mark of 98 in
arithmetic, she wanted to know who had
gotten the other two points.

— *Sam Levenson*

Much that passes for education . . . is not
education at all but ritual. The fact is that
we are being educated when we know it least.

— *David P. Gardner*

An anxious mother was questioning
[Princeton University president] Woodrow
Wilson closely about what Princeton
could do for her son. "Madam," the
exasperated Wilson replied, "we guarantee
satisfaction or you will get your son back."

—*James C. Humes*

It is one of the great pleasures of a student's life to buy a heap of books at the beginning of the autumn. Here, he fancies, are all the secrets.

—Robert Lynd

TEACHER: "Spell 'straight.'"
PUPIL: "S-T-R-A-I-G-H-T."
TEACHER: "Correct. What does it mean?"
PUPIL: "Without ginger ale."

—Lewis and Faye Copeland

A third-grader came home from school recently and announced jubilantly that his class had a substitute teacher. "And she has only two rules we have to follow," he said, "sit down and shut up."

—*Mack McGinnis*

Sign on a high school bulletin board in Dallas: Free every Monday through Friday— knowledge. Bring your own containers.

—*E. C. McKenzie*

The self-taught man seldom knows anything accurately, and he does not know a tenth as much as he could have known if he had worked under teachers, and besides, he brags, and is the means of fooling other thoughtless people into doing as he himself has done.

—*Mark Twain*

One of the troubles of the day, observes
Mr. C. N. Peace, is that once we came upon
the little red schoolhouse, whereas now we
come upon the little-read schoolboy.

—*Bennett Cerf*

The carefully fostered theory that
schoolwork can be made easy and enjoyable
breaks down as soon as anything, however
trivial, has to be learned.

—*Agnes Repplier*

A mountaineer took his son to a school to enroll him. "My boy's after larnin', what d'ya have?" he asked the teacher.

"We offer English, trigonometry, spelling, etc.," she replied.

"Well, give him some of that thar trigernometry; he's the worst shot in the family."

—*Lewis and Faye Copeland*

Every schoolmaster, after the age of forty-nine,
is inclined to flatulence, is apt to swallow
frequently, and to puff.

—*Harold Nicolson*

I am not authorized to fire substitute teachers.
I am not authorized to fire substitute teachers.
I am not authorized to fire . . .

—*Bart Simpson*

One of my third-graders kept the classroom informed on the progress of the renovations to his family's house. After it was all finished, he shared how much his mother and father were enjoying the new room. "There's a fireplace now, and my mom and dad like to sit in front of it and drink wine and be lovey-dovey."

A few months later when the parents came to school for parents' night . . . I noticed that mom was pregnant!

—*Jean Sharkey Funkhouser*

As the youngsters grow attached to their teachers and classmates . . . they can finally say goodbye to their mothers without reenacting the death scene from *Camille*.

—*Sue Mittenthal*

Teaching has ruined more American novelists than drink.

—*Gore Vidal*

An English prof at Vassar was impressing upon his freshman class the advantages of acquiring a large vocabulary. "Say a word out loud to yourself five times," he advised, "and it will be yours for life." A pert frosh in the front row closed her eyes and breathed ecstatically, "Walter, Walter, Walter, Walter, Walter . . ."

—*Bennett Cerf*

TEACHER: "I'd like to go an entire day without scolding you!"

STUDENT: "Well, teacher, you certainly have my permission."

—*James E. Myers*

A teacher's constant task is to take a roomful of live wires and see to it that they're grounded.

—*E. C. Mckenzie*

A kindergarten teacher . . . was telling her new students the rules of the classroom. When she got to the instructions about how to take care of their bodily needs, she told them that if they needed to go to the bathroom, they should just raise their hand with two fingers showing.

Immediately, one of the new students raised his hand. He said, "Miss Davies, I just don't understand how that's gonna help."

—*Daniel Kelly,* Warning! Cute Kid Stories Ahead!

CHARLIE MCCARTHY: "I can't take this schoolwork anymore—it's driving me nuts."
EDGAR BERGEN: "Well, Charlie, I'm sorry, but
hard work never killed anyone."
CHARLIE MCCARTHY: "Still, there's no use in
taking chances."

—*Gene Perret*

The truth is that I am enslaved . . . in one vast
love affair with seventy children.

—*Sylvia Ashton-Warner*

One teacher recently retired with a
half-million dollars after thirty years of
working hard, caring, dedicating herself,
and totally immersing herself in the problems
of the students. That gave her $50. The
rest came from the death of a rich uncle.

—*Milton Berle*

All through his education, the only time he
wasn't late for school was when he was absent.

—*Gene Perret*

"And how do you like going to school, Roger?" a kindly lady inquired of a very small lad.

"Oh, I like the going all right," the boy replied, "and I like coming back too. It's having to stay after I get there that bothers me."

—*Jacob M. Braude*

A self-taught man usually has a poor teacher and a worse student.

—*Henny Youngman*

A young woman named Murphy was the teacher of the kindergarten grade in a Massachusetts school. She had taught her class to repeat together the Twenty-third Psalm. As the little voices chorused out, she seemed somewhere to detect a false note. She heard the children one by one, until at last she came across one little boy who was concluding the psalm with the words, "Surely good Miss Murphy shall follow me all the days of my life."

—Edmund Fuller

I expect you'll be becoming a schoolmaster, sir.
That's what most of the gentlemen does, sir,
that gets sent down for indecent behavior.

—*Evelyn Waugh*, Decline and Fall

Children of distinction: The kid from
Texas who got all the way to the finals of a
national spelling bee but then lost out
because he couldn't spell "small."

—*Bennett Cerf*

A teacher entered the classroom and noticed a girl student sitting with her feet in the aisle and chewing gum.

"Ethel," exclaimed the teacher, "take that gum out of your mouth and put your feet in."

—*Lewis and Faye Copeland*

Everybody is ignorant, only on different subjects.

—*Will Rogers*

One happy first-grader came to school and ran up to his teacher to announce that he had a new sister. The teacher said, "Wonderful . . . and how much did she weigh?"

The lad replied: "It's not important because she didn't cost anything. My mom laid her."

—*James E. Myers*

I still remember my college days— all four of them.

—*Henny Youngman*

My ten-year-old was very appreciative of the powers-that-be who closed Stillwater's schools due to the weather.

"Mom, who is in charge of closing the schools?" he asked the second morning—still snuggling under his covers.

"Well," I explained, "the superintendent of your school . . . made that decision."

"Mom," he said, in all earnest, "he's a good man."

—*Daniel Kelly,* Warning! Cute Kid Stories Ahead!

When the examination was over, the
teacher in a mountain school told her pupils
to write a pledge that they had neither
received nor given help. One gangling youth,
who had squirmed in dismay and mopped a
bewildered brow throughout the ordeal wrote:
"I ain't received no help in this matter,
and God knows I couldn't have gave any."

—*Harry B. Otis*

Academic vows: poverty, bibliography,
and jargon.

—*Leo Rosten*

I saw nothing unusual in the teacher's lounge.
I saw nothing unusual in the teacher's lounge.
I saw nothing unusual in the teach . . .

—*Bart Simpson*

We need programs that will teach athletes
how to spell "jump shot" rather than
how to shoot it.

—*Larry Hawkins*

It is when the gods hate a man with
uncommon abhorrence that they drive
him into the profession of a schoolmaster.

—*Seneca*

FIRST STUDENT: "How old is Professor Greene?"
SECOND STUDENT: "Pretty old. They say he used
to teach Shakespeare."

—*Mildred Meiers and Jack Knapp*

Education: The path from cocky ignorance to
miserable uncertainty.

—*Mark Twain*

Many boys are flunking geometry. They just don't know the angles.

—*E. C. McKenzie*

Governor Jerry Apodaca visited the elementary school in East Plains, New Mexico, and offered to answer questions from the children. One first-grade boy put up his hand and asked, "Can we go outside and play?"

—*Harry B. Otis*

For every student with a spark
of brilliance, there are about ten
with ignition trouble.

—Milton Berle

A good teacher has been defined
as one who makes himself
progressively unnecessary.

—Thomas J. Carruthers

FATHER: "Tell me how school went today. How do you like it?"

BILLY: "It's hard to like a place that's haunted, dad."

FATHER: "Haunted! What are you talking about?"

BILLY: "It's that new teacher of mine . . . she keeps talking about the school spirit!"

—*James E. Myers*

TEACHER: "Now Billy, what do we mean by plural?"

BILLY: "By plural we mean it's the same thing, only more of it."

The aim of education should be to teach the child to think, not what to think.

—*John Dewey*

My belief is that the last thing a good teacher
wants to do is to teach outside the classroom;
certainly my own vision of bliss halfway
through a term is solitary confinement
in a soundproof cell.

—*Jacques Barzun*

What a teacher doesn't say . . . is a telling
part of what a student hears.

—*Maurice Natanson*

A good teacher, like a good entertainer,
first must hold his audience's attention.
Then he can teach his lesson.

—*Hendrik John Clarke*

What's a' your jargon o' your schools,
Your Latin names for horns and stools;
If honest Nature made you fools,
What sairs your grammars?

—*Robert Burns*

It is tiresome to hear education discussed,
tiresome to educate, and tiresome to
be educated.

—*William Lamb*

TEACHER: "I hope I didn't see you looking at
Fred's book, Tommy."

TOMMY: "I hope you didn't, too, sir.

—*Lewis and Faye Copeland*

Teacher's True Story

Andy was having a rough day on the playground. He kept climbing and falling, climbing and falling. More frustrated than hurt with his scrapes and bruises, he proclaimed, "I wish there was no such thing as hard."

—Pamela Bartels

[My first-grade son] was eager to boast . . . of his new accomplishment: knowing the whole Pledge of Allegiance.

He said it: "I pledge allegiance to the flag of the United States of America, and to the republic for which it stands—one nation, under God, indivisible, with liberty and justice for all. You may sit down."

—*Daniel Kelly*, Warning! Cute Kid Stories Ahead!

You send your child to the schoolmaster, but
'tis the schoolboys who educate him.

—*Ralph Waldo Emerson*

I'll never learn how to spell. The teacher
keeps changing the words.

—*Henny Youngman*

A school started a sex education program, and on the first day little Megan came home and told her mother, "We learned how to make babies today."

Stunned at the speed with which the subject was being taught, her mother asked, "All right, tell me how you make babies."

Megan said, "You drop the 'y' and add 'i-e-s'!"

—*Milton Berle*

But, good gracious, you've got to educate him first. You can't expect a boy to be vicious till he's been to a good school.

—*Saki (H. H. Munro)*

The teacher told my kid, "An apple a day keeps the doctor away." He said, "What do you got for cops?"

—*Rodney Dangerfield*

Teaching is not a lost art, but the regard
for it is a lost tradition.

—*Jacques Barzun*

Education: That which reveals to the wise,
conceals from the stupid, the vast limits
of their knowledge.

—*Mark Twain*

When the pupils were assigned the task of writing an essay on "The most beautiful thing I ever saw," the least aesthetic young man in the class handed in his paper first with astonishing speed. It was short and to the point—"The most beautiful thing I ever saw was too beautiful for words."

—*Edmund Fuller*

The chief object of education is not to learn
things but to unlearn things.

—*G. K. Chesterton*

Sixty years ago I knew everything; now I know
nothing; education is a progressive discovery
of our own ignorance.

—*Will Durant*

The day of a big snowstorm, the country schoolteacher felt called upon to warn her charges against playing too long in the snow. She said, "Now, children, you must be careful about colds and overexposure. I had a darling little brother only seven years old. One day he went out in the snow with his new sled and caught cold. Pneumonia set in and three days later he died."

The room was silent and then a youngster in the back row raised his hand and asked, "Where's his sled?"

—*Edmund Fuller*

The teacher of a high school class in the
fundamentals of economics led the discussion
around to the population explosion. "Certain
levels of our society reproduce much more
frequently than others," he pointed out.
"What people would you guess reproduce
the most?" One bright student
answered, "Women."

—*Bennett Cerf*

When you wish to instruct, be brief; that
men's minds take in quickly what you say,
learn its lesson, and retain it faithfully.
Every word that is unnecessary only pours
over the side of the brimming mind.

—*Cicero*

I am quite sure that in the hereafter
she will take me by the hand and lead me
to my proper seat.

—*Bernard Baruch, about one of his early teachers*

I will not make flatulent noises in class.
I will not make flatulent noises in class.
I will not make flatulent . . .

—*Bart Simpson*

TEACHER: "Willie, how do you define
ignorance?"
WILLIE: "It's when you don't know something and somebody finds it out."

—*Lewis and Faye Copeland*

I am a first-grade teacher. Recently, I had a miscarriage. Since my students had been aware of my pregnancy, I needed to explain that the baby had died. After I had read a book that covered explaining miscarriages to children, I set out to do it properly. After my explanation, I received the following four questions:

"Did you see the baby?"

"Did it hurt?"

"Is your baby in heaven?"

"When is the Christmas party again?"

—*Daniel Kelly*, Warning! Cute Kid Stories Ahead!

A teacher at my son's grade school announced that she was engaged and the entire school was delighted. Everybody liked this particular teacher. One boy wrote her a note:

Dear Mrs. Albright:
I sure do hope you have a happy and sexfull life.
Your student and friend,
Howard Viel

—James E. Myers

Tots who started kindergarten at a certain elementary school came home the first day with a special note for mom from the teachers which read, in part: "If you promise not to believe everything your child says happens at school, I'll promise not to believe everything he says happens at home."

—*Harry B. Otis*

The secret of teaching is to appear
to have known all your life what you
learned this afternoon.

— Anonymous

On arriving home from school, a little boy announced, "My math teacher is crazy."

"Why?" his mother asked.

"Yesterday," he replied, "she told us that five is four plus one; today she is telling us that five is three plus two."

When I was a first-grade art teacher, one of the classes was a group of children who were obviously not as well off as some of the other kiddos. Anyway, this one little girl that you just wanted to take home and feed for about four years—she looked so skinny—had drawn this really nice little [Christmas] picture . . . and you could see Mary, and you see Joseph and the shepherds—but . . . Joseph had this humongous frown on his face.

I said: "Well . . . what's the matter with Joseph?"

And she said: "Mary just told him they're gonna have another baby."

—*Daniel Kelly*, Warning! Cute Kid Stories Ahead!

Harvard University is conceded to be one of the nation's greatest storehouses of knowledge, and its onetime president, the late Charles W. Eliot, had a ready explanation. "We're adding more knowledge every semester," he declared. "The freshman bring us so much of it—and the seniors take away so little!"

—*Bennett Cerf*

There must be such a thing as a child with average ability, but you can't find a parent who will admit that it is his child.

—*Thomas Bailey*

Who walks in the classroom cool and slow?
Who calls his English teacher Daddy-O?
Charlie Brown, He's a clown . . .

—*Jerry Leiber and Mike Stoller, "Charlie Brown"*

CRAZY THINGS KIDS WRITE
ON TESTS

The blood circulates through the body by flowing down one leg and up the other.

Often when people are drown, you can revive them by pounding them in the belly, but not too hard. This is called resurrection.

A city purifies its water supply by filtering the water, then forcing it through an aviator.

We do not raise silkworms in the United States, because we get our silk from rayon. He is a larger worm and gives more silk.

When teacher asked in what part of the world the most ignorant people were to be found, a small boy volunteered quickly, "In New York."

The teacher was amazed, and questioned the lad as to where he had obtained such information.

"Well," he replied, "the geography says that's where the population is most dense."

—*Lewis and Faye Copeland*

Education is a wonderful thing. If you couldn't
sign your name you'd have to pay cash.

—*Rita Mae Brown*

We had a teacher in school who hated
kids—he caught me reading a comic book in
class and snatched it away from me. "You'll
get this back at the end of the semester."

"Why, is it gonna take you that long to
read it?"

—*Bill Cosby*

For every person who wants to teach there are approximately thirty who don't want to learn—much.

—*W. C. Sellar and R. J. Yeatman*

Stand firm in your refusal to remain conscious during algebra. In real life, I assure you, there is no such thing as algebra.

—*Fran Leibowitz*

A bright little lassie in Lawrence
Used language that came out in tawrence,
Till informed by the teacher,
"Your manners, dear creature,
Are worse than your scholarship wawrence."

—Bennett Cerf

Children are unpredictable. You never
know what inconsistency they're going
to catch you in next.

—Franklin P. Jones

Little Billy brought home his report card. His mother took him to task for all the low grades. Little Billy responded, "It's got its good side too. You know darn well I'm not cheating!"

—*Milton Berle*

This punishment is not boring and pointless. This punishment is not boring and pointless. This punishment is not boring . . .

—*Bart Simpson*

I was casting kids . . . for our annual
Christmas play, and I was giving out choices,
such as shepherd, lamb, villager.

One five-year-old boy couldn't decide, so
I said, "Luke, you can be a villager."

He said, "Okay"—and ran over to his
parents. Very excited, he said to them, "Guess
what! I get to be a mini-van!"

—*Daniel Kelly*, Warning! Cute Kid Stories Ahead!

Children of distinction: The little girl who assured her teacher, "Of course I know how to spell banana. I just never know when to stop."

—*Bennett Cerf*

The only reason I always try to meet and know the parents better is because it helps me to forgive the children.

—*Louis Johannot*

The mediocre teacher tells.
The good teacher explains.
The superior teacher demonstrates.
The great teacher inspires.

—*William Arthur Ward*

Education is . . . hanging around until
you've caught on.

—*Robert Frost*

A teacher was having trouble teaching arithmetic to one little boy. So she asked, "If you reached in your right pocket and found a nickel, and you reached in your left pocket and found another one, what would you have?" "Somebody else's pants," said the little boy.

—*Loyal Jones*

A five-year-old's definition of
nursery school: "A place where they
teach children who hit, not to hit,
and children who don't hit, to hit back."

—*James E. Myers*

If we succeed in giving the love of learning,
the learning itself is sure to follow.

—*Sir John Lubbock*

"All right, Eustace," the teacher said to the fifth-grader, "let's see you count."

Holding out his hand, Eustace counted off the digits. "One, two, three, four, five."

Smiling, the teacher said, "Very good, but can you count any higher?"

Lifting his hand over his head, the boy started over again.

—*Jeff Rovin*

I'm never going to be a movie star. But then,
in all probability, Liz Taylor is never going
to teach first and second grade.

—*Mary J. Wilson*

Education cannot be conferred.
Whether in school or out, learning is a
do-it-yourself proposition.

—*Wheeler McMillen*

True Story

The school board official was picking his way carefully across the schoolyard one winter day. After several days of hard frost there was a light coating of snow, and the ground was treacherous. Suddenly his legs shot from under him and the official, briefcase, and hat went flying. A small boy ran up to him. "Thank you, Sir!" he shouted.

"What do you mean—thank you?" demanded the official.

"You've found our slide!" said the boy.

—Rosy Border

The mind grows by what it feeds on.

—*J. G. Holland*

The teacher asked, "Tell me, Johnny, if I had nine apples and there were twelve children, how would I divide them equally?" Johnny thought for a moment, then replied happily, "Make applesauce!"

—*Helen Rudin*

Thinking is the hardest work there is,
which is the probable reason why so
few engage in it.

—*Henry Ford*

Knowledge comes, but wisdom lingers.

—*Tennyson*

Reasons to Be a Teacher

You want to get home before the rush hour
starts, even if you have to drive a
1968 Dodge Dart to do it.

You want your summers free so you
can scrape together a living by driving a cab,
tending bar, and selling Fuller brushes.

—Art Peterson

"Bobby, this is about the worst composition I have ever read. I can't believe you alone could make so many errors."

"You're right, Miss Brown! Dad helped me write it."

—*Paul McClure*

If you think that one individual can't make a difference in the world, consider what one cigar can do in a nine-room house.

—*Bill Vaughn*

Sam had just completed his first day at school. "What did you learn today?" asked his mother. "Not enough," said Sammy. "I have to go back tomorrow."

—*Joseph Rosenbloom*

A lazy schoolboy lets his father do his homework, but a bright one helps his father with it.

—*Evan Esar*

What Will Happen During Your First Year of Teaching?

You will become well-known as an easy touch for candy sales, car-wash tickets, and walkathon contributions.

A seasoned teacher will say to you, "You couldn't possibly have that many A and B students."

Three parents will tell you their children never had a bit of trouble until this year.

— Art Peterson

One day, after a group discussion about family celebrations, one little boy in my preschool class raised his hand. He said, "My family celebrates Lent." A girl sitting next to him said "What's that?" He very seriously replied, "You know, that fuzzy stuff in your dryer."

— *Valeka Petersen*

Science is simply common sense at its best.

—*T. H. Huxley*

TEACHER: "What is an Indian's wife called?"
GIRL: "A squaw, miss."
TEACHER: "Quite right. And what are Indian babies called?"
BOY: "Squawkers?"

—Michael Kilgarriff

The Great Cliché:
This will definitely be on the exam.
The Truth: Will somebody please wake up?

—Art Peterson

Jimmie carried the following excuse to his teacher the next morning: "Please excuse Jimmie from being absent. He has a new baby brother. It was not his fault."

—*Lewis and Faye Copeland*

How to be a good *teacher:* Teach the basic subject. Have an atmosphere conducive to learning. Hold the student accountable for progress. Have performance standards.

—*Colonel Patrick Harrington, USMC*

Latin's a dead language
As dead as dead can be;
It killed off all the Romans,
And now it's killing me.

—*Michael Kilgarriff*

In some high schools, teachers have a lot of
respect for their students. That's because the
students are older than they are!

—*Milton Berle*

The better part of every man's education
is that which he gives himself.

—*J. R. Lowell*

Minds are like parachutes. They only
function when they are open.

—*Thomas Dewar*

What is done by the family in the home environment has far greater influence on children than anything a school can do or undo. Unstable homes, with parents in motion day and night and over weekends make the school's job difficult, if not impossible.

—*Terrel H. Bell, U.S. Commissioner of Education*

Wisdom is one treasure that no thief can touch.

—*Japanese proverb*

TEACHER: "If I had fifty apples in my right hand and thirty apples in my left hand, what would I have?"

DEBBY: "Big hands."

—*Rosy Border*

A lecturer often makes you feel dumb at one end and numb at the other.

—*Evan Esar*

A little girl arrived at kindergarten all out of breath with excitement.

"Why, what's the matter?" asked her teacher.

"We've got a new baby at our house," she replied. "Won't you come and see it?"

"Oh, thanks!" said the teacher. "but I think I had better wait until your mother is better."

"It's all right," said the girl. "You don't have to be afraid—it's not catching."

—*Lewis and Faye Copeland*

What the good teacher has is not necessarily more knowledge than his student, but rather a superior competence to inquire and to be reflective.

—*Joseph Schwad*

The Great Cliché: Don't worry about it.
It won't be on the exam.
The Truth: I can't do this problem either.

—*Art Peterson*

One day in school, the teacher wrote on the blackboard, "I ain't had no fun at all last week." She turned to her class and said, "Now, what should I do to correct that?"

A shy student stood up and replied meekly, "Maybe you should get a boyfriend."

—*Helen Rudin*

Children have more need of models than of critics.

—*Joubert*

BILLY: "I got a hundred in school today."
MOTHER: "That's wonderful, Billy. What did
            you get a hundred in?"
BILLY: "Two things. I got fifty in spelling
            and fifty in arithmetic."

—Joseph Rosenbloom

When one teacher told his class to write the
longest sentence they could compose, a bright
spark wrote: "Imprisonment for Life"!

—Michael Kilgarriff

"You failed history? When I was your age, it was my best subject."

"When you were my age, what had happened?"

—Milton Berle

Good teachers never teach anything. What they do is create the conditions under which learning takes place.

—S. I. Hayakawa

"Mary," said the teacher, "I'd like you to come up to the map and point out Cuba to me."

"Yes, sir," Mary said, and pointed to the island.

"Very good. Now, Alexander, tell us who discovered Cuba."

The boy replied, "Mary, sir."

—*Jeff Rovin*

Read! Read something every day.
Discipline yourself to a regular schedule of
reading. In fifteen minutes a day you can
read twenty books a year.

—*Wilfred Peterson*

Q: Why is the school basketball court
always so soggy?
A: Because the players are always dribbling.

—*Rosy Border*

A father, looking over his son's
report cards notes, "One thing in your
favor, with these grades you couldn't
possibly be cheating."

— *Anonymous*

Sign in a Vassar math class:
Girls, watch your figures.

—*Helen Rudin*

LOGIC

Japanese students spend 240 days a year in school; 85 percent of this time is spent on instruction. American students spend 180 days a year in school, 25 percent of it on instruction. Therefore, it follows that:

a.   Education has nothing to do with winning world wars.

b. The number of hours Japanese students spend studying is roughly equivalent to the number of hours American students spend watching MTV.

c. We will soon be able to catch up to the Japanese with a crash program that increases the number of school days to 410 days a year.

— Art Peterson

JUNIOR: "Pop, I can tell you how to save money."

FATHER: "That's fine. How?"

JUNIOR: "Remember you promised me $5 if I got passing grades?"

FATHER: "Yes."

JUNIOR: "Well, you don't have to pay me."

—*Joseph Rosenbloom*

There is only one thing that costs more than
education today, the lack of it.

—Anonymous

TEACHER: "A fool can ask more questions than
a wise man can answer."

STUDENT: "No wonder so many of us flunk
our exams."

MOTHER: (teaching her son arithmetic): "Now take the Smith family— there's mommy, daddy, and the baby. How many does that make?"

BRIGHT SON: "Two and one to carry."

—*Lewis and Faye Copeland*

Education, to be successful, must not only inform but inspire.

—*T. Sharper Knowlson*

"Sir, I didn't deserve the grade you gave
me on this test."
"Do you know a lower one?"

—*Milton Berle*

TEACHER: "Why is it said that lightning never
strikes the same place twice?"
ROY: "Because after it's struck once, the
same place isn't there anymore!"

—*Michael Kilgarriff*

215

A smart mother suggests that her child
bring an apple to his teacher; a smarter
mother suggests that he bring a
couple of aspirins.

—*Evan Esar*

Thinking is like loving or dying.
Each of us must do it for himself.

—*Josiah Royce*

For some reason, everyone but Lenore got the wrong answer on the science test.

"Tell me," the teacher asked her after returning the papers, "how did you know that heat causes objects to expand, and cold causes them to shrink?"

"Because I'm no dope," she said. "In the summer, when it's hot, the days are longer. And in the winter, when it's cold, they're shorter."

—*Jeff Rovin*

HARRY: "I don't think my woodshop teacher likes me much."

GARY: "What makes you think that?"

HARRY: "He's teaching me to make a coffin!"

—*Rosy Border*

FATHER: "Well, son, how are your marks?"

SON: "Under water."

FATHER: "What do you mean?"

SON: "Below 'C' level."

—*Joseph Rosenbloom*

Learning is like rowing upstream,
not to advance is to drop back.

—Chinese proverb

Some lecturers talk in their sleep,
but most talk in other people's sleep.

—Evan Esar

A teacher was giving her class a little weekly talk on painting, illustrated by reproductions of famous pictures. "Sir Joshua Reynolds," she said, "was able to change a smiling face into a frowning one with a single stroke of the brush."

"Huh," little Johnnie was heard to mutter, "my maw kin do that!"

—Lewis and Faye Copeland

It is not the IQ but the I WILL that is most important in education.

— Anonymous

TEACHER: "Why was the period between A.D. 500 and A.D. 1000 known as the Dark Ages?"

HEATHER: "Because those were the days of the (k)nights."

— Michael Kilgarriff

Even a professor soon discovers
how little he knows when a child
begins asking questions.

— Anonymous

Puberty is the period when students
stop asking questions and begin to
question answers.

— Anonymous

Looking over at the least competent speller in the class, the English teacher said, "Here's an easy one, Rufus. Spell 'weather.'"

Pulling at his chin, Rufus said, "W-E-T-H-O-R," and smiled.

Sighing, the teacher said, "Rufus, that's the worst spell of weather we've had here for quite some time."

—*Jeff Rovin*

TEACHER: "You missed school yesterday, Debby, didn't you?"

DEBBY: "No, sir—I didn't miss it one bit!"

—Rosy Border

A guide to classroom discipline: Tell the class to pay attention while you explain the new miracle cure for zits.

—Art Peterson

Teacher's True Story

Trying to get Kyle to eat healthy, I said, "Eat your peas. It will make your eyes sparkle." Joey overheard and blurted out, "Teacher—my cat's eyes sparkle!"

I replied, "That's nice. Does your cat eat peas?" "No," responded Joey, "but he drinks water out of the toilet."

—Martha Gillham

Experience is a great teacher, and sometimes
a pretty teacher is a great experience.

—Evan Esar

If the cost of education continues to rise,
education will become as expensive
as ignorance.

—Phi Delta Kappan

A Texas lad rushed home from kindergarten class and insisted his mother buy him a set of pencils, holsters, and a gun belt.

"Whatever for, dear?" his mother asked. "You're not going to tell me you need them for school?"

"Yes, I do," he replied. "Teacher said that tomorrow she's going to teach us how to draw."

— *Joseph Rosenbloom*

Grace, a five-year-old, returned from her first day in kindergarten. Grace's mother asked, "How old is your teacher?"

Grace said, "I'm not sure. She's either an early lady or a late teenager!"

—*Milton Berle*

Encourage spontaneity . . . by regularly scheduling creative activities.

—*Art Peterson*

TEACHER: "Sally, your handwriting gets worse each day you're in this class."

SALLY: "Gosh, Mr. Smithers, if I wrote any better you would start noticing my bad spelling."

—Helen Rudin

There are two types of students who ask to do extra credit: those who do not need it and those who will not complete it.

—Art Peterson

LIBRARIAN: "Sh-hh-hh! The people next to you can't read."

STUDENT: "What a shame! I've been reading ever since I was six years old."

—*Joseph Rosenbloom*

It is the supreme art of the teacher to awaken joy in creative expression and knowledge.

—*Albert Einstein*

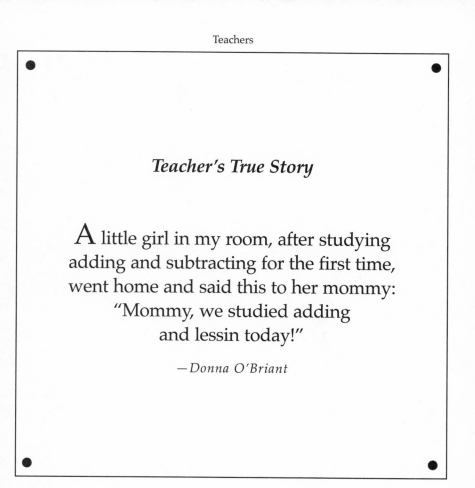

Teacher's True Story

A little girl in my room, after studying
adding and subtracting for the first time,
went home and said this to her mommy:
"Mommy, we studied adding
and lessin today!"

—Donna O'Briant

The teacher was trying to impress upon her pupils the importance of doing right at all times, and to bring out the answer, "Bad habits," she inquired: "What is it that we find so easy to get into and so hard to get out of?" There was silence for a moment and then one little fellow answered "Bed."

—*Lewis and Faye Copeland*

The lecturer who is full of his subject is usually very slow in emptying himself.

—Evan Esar

Unfortunately, the popular English teacher came down with the flu and had to be hospitalized. There, she received countless get-well cards addressed to the ill literate.

—Jeff Rovin

The more whimsical and cantankerous a teacher's grading system, the less the chance of her being replaced by an Apple II computer.

—Art Peterson

Inside every C+ student is a B- student trying to get out.

—Art Peterson

Teacher's True Story

Our routine for show-and-tell involves standing in a circle and each child hiding their special item behind their back until it is their time to share. As I announced Emily's turn, Benjamin shouted out, " know what she has! She has a diarrhea!" Not knowing for sure, I was a little relieved when she pulled out her diary.

— Amy Brown

Taking her kindergarten class to the petting zoo, Mrs. Ganio gave each child a turn identifying the animals. Finally it was young Bess's turn. Pointing to a deer, the teacher asked, "Now what is the name of that animal?"

Bess looked long and hard, but was unable to come up with an answer.

"Think," the teacher encouraged. "What does your mommy call your daddy at home?"

Suddenly the girl's face brightened. "So that's what a horse's ass looks like?"

—*Jeff Rovin*

TEACHER: "Where are the Andes, Debby?"
DEBBY: "At the end of the armies, Ma'am."

—Rosy Border

There will rarely be genuine and healthy
laughter in a classroom unless the teacher
can laugh at a number of things in general,
and at himself in particular.

—Anonymous

More people than ever before are graduated
but not educated.

—Robert Gunderson

TEACHER: "Jimmy, use this book wisely. You
will discover it will do half your
work,"
JIMMY: "Great! I'll take two."

—Helen Rudin

The college professor got up from behind his desk and walked over to a student sitting in the front row and asked, "Martin, do you know the capital of Alaska?"

The student said, "Juneau!"

The professor growled, "Sure I know, but I'm asking you."

—Helen Rudin

Small boy to father: "There's a special PTA meeting tonight; just you, my teacher, and the principal."

—The Amplifier, *Mansfield, Ohio*

In any classroom, the percentage of B-, C-, and D- grades is directly proportional to the teacher's need to remain free of hassles with kids and parents.

—*Art Peterson*

Back in the old days it was the student rather than the teacher who had to explain why they could not read.

—Cy N. Peace

Lecturers should remember that the capacity of the mind to absorb is limited to what the seat can endure.

—Evan Esar

CRAZY THINGS KIDS WRITE ON TESTS

The future of "I give" is "I take."

To prevent head colds, use an agonizer to spray into the nose until it drips into the throat.

Heredity means that . . . if your grandpa
didn't have any children, then your daddy
probably wouldn't have had any, and
neither would you, probably.

The climate is hottest next to the Creator.

TEACHER: "Johnny, can you tell me what a waffle is?"

JOHNNY: "Yes'm, it's a pancake with a non-skid tread."

—*Lewis and Faye Copeland*

Discipline is a matter of being able to get attention when you want it.

—*From the book* Teacher

Why study? The more we know, the more we forget. The more we forget, the less we know. The less we know, the less we forget. The less we forget, the more we know. Why study?

—*Milton Berle*

For the harmony of two, be they friends or teacher-pupil, the patience of one is necessary.

—*M. Dale Baughman*

The arithmetic teacher had written 10.9 on the blackboard, and had then rubbed out the decimal point to show the effect of multiplying this number by ten.

"Johnson," he asked, "Where is the decimal point now?"

"On the eraser, sir!" came the reply.

—*Michael Kilgarriff*

It is not uncommon for someone in our society to sit for 14,000 hours in a classroom and still not know for sure what a sentence is.

— Art Peterson

Knowledge is like money. If you keep quiet about it, people will think you've got more than you have.

— Anonymous

Teacher's True Story

Little Tori gave me a great big hug when she came to class one morning.

I noticed that she smelled real nice and told her so. She replied, "Thanks! I put on some of my dad's boyfume."

— *Amy Brown*

Knowledge is like money. If you keep quiet
about it, people will think you've got
more than you have.

—Anonymous

TEACHER: "Sarah, what was the first thing
James the First did on coming to the
throne?"
SARAH: "He sat down, miss."

—Michael Kilgarriff

The whole reason for juvenile delinquency is mental unemployment.

—Jackie Gleason

Tales are told of the teacher who talks to the furniture, tales substantiated by students who have passed his room and heard, "Table Three, will you be quiet, Table Three."

—Art Peterson

Education makes a people easy to lead,
but difficult to drive; easy to govern,
but impossible to enslave.

—Lord Brougham

TEACHER: "You mustn't fight, Harry. You
should learn to give and take."
HARRY: "I did, sir. He took my Mars bar and I
gave him a black eye!"

—Rosy Border

The secret of education lies in
respecting the pupil.

—*Ralph Waldo Emerson*

A child prodigy is a youngster who is too
young to be as old as he is.

—*Evan Esar*

TEACHER: "How old were you on your last birthday?"

PUPIL: "Seven."

TEACHER: "How old will you be on your next birthday?"

PUPIL: "Nine."

TEACHER: "That's impossible."

PUPIL: "No, it isn't, teacher. I'm eight today."

—*Joseph Rosenbloom*

TEACHER: "Barbara, finish off this proverb: one good turn . . ."
BARBARA: "One good turn gives you all the blankets!"

—*Michael Kilgarriff*

Nowadays, when a speaker tells the graduates that the future is theirs—is that a promise or a threat?

—*Milton Berle*

A teacher asked the class to name the states of the United States. One child responded so promptly and accurately as to bring forth this comment from the teacher: "You did very well—much better than I could have done at your age."

"Yes, you could," said the child consolingly, "there were only thirteen then."

—*Lewis and Faye Copeland*

Good teachers cost a lot, but poor
teachers cost a lot more.

—*Evan Esar*

The irony of teaching: The good kids you have
to pass to the next grade, while the bad kids
end up spending another year with you.

—*Helen Rudin*

If they made hooky a major, the dropout rate
would go down to zero.

—Milton Berle

TEACHER: "Sammy, please give me an example
            of a double negative."
SAMMY: "I don't know none."
TEACHER: "Correct, thank you!"

—Joseph Rosenbloom

TEACHER: "What do you know about the
Dead Sea?"

GARRY: "I didn't even know it was ill?"

—Rosy Border

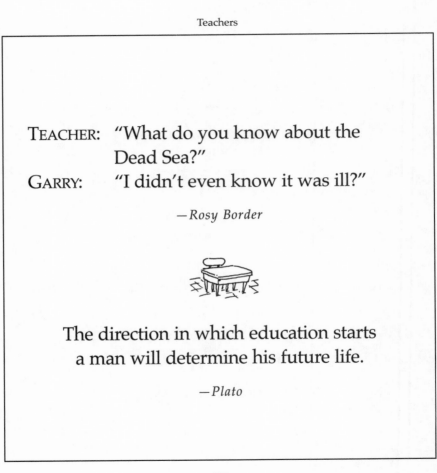

The direction in which education starts
a man will determine his future life.

—Plato

The aspiring psychiatrists were attending their first class on emotional extremes.

"Just to establish some parameters," said the professor, "Mr. Nichols: What is the opposite of joy?"

"Sadness," said the student.

"And the opposite of depression, Ms. Biggs?"

"Elation."

"How about the opposite of woe, Mr. Wilson?"

"I believe that's giddyap," the student replied.

—Jeff Rovin

Education has finally come up with an
effective way to deal with high school
students who are habitual troublemakers.
They graduate them!

—*Helen Rudin*

A schoolteacher handles many more
children than a parent, and is given two
months' vacation every year to recuperate.

—*Evan Esar*

A schoolteacher who had been telling a class
of small pupils the story of the discovery of
America by Columbus ended with: "And all
this happened more than 400 years ago."
A little boy, his eyes wide open with wonder,
said, after a moment's thought: "Gee!
What a memory you've got."

—*Lewis and Faye Copeland*

To teach is to learn twice over.

—*Joseph Joubert*

If teachers of fifty years ago were
suddenly resurrected, only June, July, and
August would be the same.

—*Paul McClure*

If he ever lives to be an adult, it'll be
a testament to his teachers' patience and
his parents' self-control!

—*Milton Berle*

TEACHER: "Doreen, I told you to write out this poem twenty times because your handwriting is so bad, and you've only written it out seventeen times."

DOREEN: "My arithmetic's bad as well, teacher."

—*Michael Kilgarriff*

Experience is a hard teacher because she gives the test first, the lesson afterward.

—*Vernon Law*

Books are not men and yet they are alive.
They are man's memory and his aspiration,
the link between his present and his past,
the tools he builds with.

—Stephen V. Benet

A college degree and a teaching certificate
define a person as a teacher, but it takes hard
work and dedication to be one.

—Paul McClure